50 Funny Fun Facts That Will Make You Laugh and Blow Your Mind

By Mihai Gingu

DISCLAIMER

This book was created with the assistance of ChatGPT, an AI language model developed by OpenAI. The facts, humor, and writing are the result of a collaboration between the author and AI technology. While every effort has been made to ensure the accuracy and quality of the content, the author takes full responsibility for the final material presented in this book.

This book is intended purely for entertainment purposes. The information contained within is not meant to be taken as professional advice or a scientifically verified source. Readers are encouraged to verify facts independently if planning to use them beyond enjoying a good laugh.

All rights to the content, including text and design, are owned by the author. Amazon.com, Kindle Direct Publishing (KDP), and any other third-party platforms or services are not liable for any errors, omissions, or inaccuracies in the book's content. Enjoy the fun facts and remember: laughter is a universal language!

A Message From the Author

Hi there, I'm Mihai!
You know that feeling when you just want to sit back, relax, and have a good laugh?
Well, that's exactly what I was looking for—but apparently, every book I wanted to read
didn't exist. So, I thought, why not create it myself?

This book is a blend of fun, laughter, and a sprinkle of surprising knowledge. It's for
anyone who loves quirky facts, a good chuckle, and maybe even a "wait, really?!"
moment. Writing this has been a journey of cracking myself up while discovering some
truly mind-blowing trivia, and now, I'm excited to share it all with you.

So, here I am—writing this book to laugh, learn, and hopefully pass that joy along to
you. Whether you're here to pick up some trivia for your next party or just to have a
lighthearted read, I hope this book becomes your go-to for a great time.
Enjoy and happy laughing!

Mihai Gingu

Table of Contents

Introduction: Laughing at the Weirdest Truths About Our World

Welcome, fellow truth-seeker and laughter enthusiast! You've just opened the door to a world filled with some of the strangest, funniest, and downright mind-boggling facts about the universe. If you're ready to laugh until your stomach hurts (or at least until you question everything you thought you knew), you've come to the right place.

Have you ever found yourself in a moment of sheer wonder, thinking, "Wait, what?" Well, this book is your golden ticket to more of those moments, and trust me, there's plenty of room for you to scratch your head and giggle along the way. From bizarre animals that breathe out of their butts to strange historical events that sound like something out of a comedy sketch, we've gathered the weirdest truths about our world for your entertainment. So buckle up, because you're in for a wild ride!

Why This Book Will Make You Question Everything
Let's be honest—everything you think you know about the world might just be wrong. This book will throw your perceptions of reality out the window and replace them with delightful, absurd facts that might leave you questioning everything from science to the way you've been pronouncing "avocado."

Want to know why cows have best friends? Curious about why you can't hum with your nose plugged? Ever wonder why sloths poop once a week but dolphins talk to each other using names? Well, you're about to find out, and you'll be laughing at how ridiculous—and yet completely true—our world really is. And don't worry, if you're not ready to re-think your entire life, these facts will at least make you a hit at your next trivia night!

How to Use This Book (Hint: With a Smile)

This isn't your typical "learn something new" book—this one's here to entertain, amuse, and maybe even make you snort with laughter at a few bizarre facts. Here's how to get the most out of it:

- **Start Anywhere** – Each chapter is filled with weirdness that'll tickle your funny bone, so feel free to dive in wherever you like. Who needs order when you're having fun?
- **Share the Laughs** – These facts are best shared! Drop them in a conversation, impress your friends, or just use them as a great icebreaker next time you're at a party.
- **Take a Moment** – Sometimes, you'll need to pause and process the insanity of what you just read. That's totally normal. Trust me, your mind is about to be blown in ways you didn't think were possible.
- **Remember to Laugh** – Most importantly, this book is here for one purpose: laughter. If you're not laughing, you might need to check your pulse (and then read another chapter).

Ready to dive into the weird and wonderful? Let's go—your mind (and your funny bone) won't know what hit it.

Chapter 1: Mind-Bending Truths About the Animal Kingdom (6 Facts)

Fur, Feathers, and Jaw-Dropping Realities

Welcome to the wild world of animals, where reality is stranger than fiction and your childhood pet may be hiding some seriously quirky secrets. Get ready to question everything you thought you knew about the animal kingdom—from penguins proposing with rocks to cows forming BFFs. Hold on tight, because nature is about to get hilariously weird!

FUNNY FUN FACT #1

Penguins Propose with Rocks

A Rock Solid Proposal

When Penguins Say "I Do," It's All About the Stones

Penguins may not have diamonds or elaborate proposals, but they sure know how to make a romantic gesture! When a male penguin is ready to woo a female, he goes on a mission to find the perfect rock. He presents it to her, and if she accepts, they become mates and start a life together. The rock, however, isn't just for decoration. It serves as a form of nesting material, which helps create a safe, cozy spot for their eggs. It's as though penguins have turned rock collection into a love language! This rock exchange is critical for their bond, and it's fascinating how animals have evolved such unique ways to court. Next time you think about romance, imagine a penguin diving into the cold waters for the perfect pebble!

Cows Have BFFs

Moo-ving with Best Friends

Cows Are Social Creatures with Friendships That Last

Cows are known for being social animals, but it might surprise you to learn that they have deep friendships, just like humans! Studies have shown that cows can form strong, emotional bonds with specific individuals within the herd. They experience distress when separated from their best friends and will actively search for each other. These friendships are more than just survival mechanisms—they are emotional connections that help cows feel secure and comfortable. In fact, cows who have BFFs tend to be calmer and more relaxed, which makes their milk production more efficient. If you ever see a cow hanging out with its best bud in the pasture, just know they're not lonely—they're in the midst of some serious cow friendship goals!

Heartfelt Oddities

Octopuses Keep Things Beating with Three Hearts

Imagine having three hearts pumping blood in your body! That's the reality for octopuses, which have a highly specialized circulatory system. Two of their hearts work together to pump blood through their gills, where oxygen is absorbed. The third heart sends oxygenated blood to the rest of the body. But here's the kicker: when an octopus swims, the heart that delivers blood to the body stops beating. This is why octopuses are known to prefer crawling on the ocean floor rather than swimming—they get tired more quickly while swimming due to this peculiar heart shutdown. Nature certainly doesn't play by the same rules for everyone, and octopuses are the perfect example of how evolution has crafted some wild and weird biological traits to help them survive in the deep sea.

Sloths Can Hold Their Breath Longer Than Dolphins

Sloth Survival Skills

The Lazy Swimmers Who Hold Their Breath for 40 Minutes

Sloths are the slow-moving, laid-back creatures of the jungle, and they take their leisurely pace to the next level. Not only are they the champions of napping, but they also hold a record for breath-holding—one that beats the dolphin! While dolphins are known for their agility in the water and can hold their breath for around 10 minutes, sloths can go a whopping 40 minutes without coming up for air. This remarkable ability is crucial for their survival because they often find themselves hanging from tree branches in shallow waters, using the technique to avoid predators. Despite their reputation for being sluggish, sloths have an ace up their sleeve when it comes to holding their breath underwater!

FUNNY FUN FACT #5

Snuggle Time at Sea

Sea Otters' Adorable Solution for Staying Close

There's nothing more adorable than a sea otter, and their social behavior takes the cake! Sea otters sleep in groups, and to ensure they don't drift away from each other, they hold hands. This behavior prevents them from getting separated while they float on their backs in the water. It's not just a cute gesture; it's a survival tactic. By holding hands, otters stay close to their friends, ensuring they are protected and not carried off by currents. It's as though otters have their own little sleepover tradition in the wild. So, if you ever see a group of otters floating hand-in-hand, just remember: they're not only snuggling—they're sticking together to make sure they don't drift apart in their dreamy aquatic slumber!

FUNNY FUN FACT #6

Role Reversal in the Sea

In the World of Seahorses, Dads Do the Baby Work

Talk about role reversal! In the fascinating world of seahorses, it's the male that takes on the task of pregnancy and childbirth. After the female seahorse transfers her eggs to the male's special brood pouch, he fertilizes them and carries them for about 10 days until they hatch. The male seahorse goes through labor and then gives birth to dozens or even hundreds of tiny seahorse babies. It's an incredible phenomenon in the animal world that challenges the typical understanding of parenting. Male seahorses are the true MVPs of the animal kingdom's parenting game, and it's not every day that you hear about a father carrying the baby for a change!

Elephants Can "Hear" Through Their Feet

Elephant Feet—The Secret Sound Detectors

Elephants Have a Keen Sense of Hearing... Through Their Feet!

Elephants might have large ears, but it turns out they can "hear" even better through their feet! These incredible creatures are able to detect sounds and vibrations from miles away by sensing seismic waves traveling through the ground. They have sensitive cells in their feet that can pick up vibrations caused by sounds, footsteps, or even storms. Elephants use this extraordinary ability to communicate with one another, keeping in touch with their herd and detecting threats from a distance. It's like their feet are built-in hearing devices. So, the next time you see an elephant with those giant ears, remember—they're not just listening with them; they've got the whole ground under their feet helping them stay tuned in!

Chapter 2: Outrageous Animal Abilities You Won't Believe (6 Facts)

Superpowers in the Wild

Forget superheroes—some animals have skills that will make even Iron Man jealous. They breathe through their butts, punch like bullets, and hold their breath longer than you'd ever want to. This chapter takes you through some of the wildest, funniest, and most jaw-dropping abilities animals have evolved, showing that in the animal kingdom, the rules of physics (and common sense) don't always apply.

A Tardigrade Can Survive in Space

Space Bear's Survival Guide

Meet the indestructible micro-creature that defies the odds.

Tardigrades, or "water bears," are some of the toughest creatures known to humanity. These microscopic organisms can survive in extreme environments that would obliterate most other life forms—like the vacuum of space! In fact, tardigrades have been sent to outer space and survived. They can endure freezing temperatures, extreme heat, radiation, and even the vacuum of space itself. When scientists talk about the most resilient creatures on Earth, the tardigrade is basically the superhero of the microscopic world. So next time you're feeling down, remember: if a tardigrade can survive space, you can definitely survive Monday.

FUNNY FUN FACT #8

A Mantis Shrimp Can Punch Like a Bullet

The Tiny Boxer with a Knockout Punch

The Mantis Shrimp: Nature's Bruce Lee.

"A mantis shrimp's punch is so fast, it hits like a bullet—literally capable of shattering glass!"

Meet the mantis shrimp, the pint-sized predator with the fastest punch in the animal kingdom. Clocking in at speeds of up to 50 miles per hour, this tiny titan's punch generates force comparable to a .22 caliber bullet. It's so powerful that it can break aquarium glass and pulverize its prey's shells in milliseconds. The real kicker? They can throw these punches thousands of times without breaking their "fists," thanks to their specialized club-like appendages. If boxing had a shrimp weight class, the mantis shrimp would be the undisputed champ!

An Elephant's Ear Is a Natural Air Conditioner

Flap Those Ears!

Elephants know how to keep cool, literally.

Elephants are equipped with huge, floppy ears, and while they may look like adorable wings, these ears have a more practical purpose: they help keep the elephants cool! The ears are packed with blood vessels that regulate their body temperature. By flapping their ears, elephants can dissipate heat and lower their body temperature. So, the next time you see an elephant flapping its ears, just know it's not just being dramatic—it's a natural air conditioner in action.

A Pistol Shrimp Can Snap Its Claws So Loudly It Can Stun Fish

A Shrimp with a Sonic Boom

When a shrimp's snap is louder than a jet engine.

The pistol shrimp may be small, but it packs a mighty punch. This shrimp can snap its claws so fast and so loud that it creates a shockwave capable of stunning fish. The snap is so powerful that it produces a sound that reaches up to 210 decibels—louder than a jet engine! Not only that, but the snap generates bubbles that reach temperatures as hot as the surface of the sun for a split second. This tiny shrimp may look unassuming, but it's the superhero of the ocean, packing a punch that would leave even the biggest fish swimming for cover.

FUNNY FUN FACT #11

A Crocodile Can't Stick Its Tongue Out

Tongue-Tied

Crocodiles are too cool to stick out their tongues.

While we humans love to stick our tongues out in moments of mischief or mockery, crocodiles aren't able to do that. The reason? Their tongues are firmly anchored to the roof of their mouths by a membrane, making it impossible for them to stick their tongues out. So, next time you're at a zoo and try to taunt a crocodile by making funny faces, just know that the only one being teased here is you. They've got a permanent poker face!

A Jellyfish Is 95% Water

See-Through But Full of Liquid

The squishy ocean creature that's mostly water—literally.

Jellyfish are one of the most bizarre creatures in the ocean. They have no bones, no heart, and no brain—yet they've survived for over 500 million years! They're 95% water, which is just one of the many reasons they're as squishy as they are. With such a watery composition, you'd think they'd just dissolve away, but jellyfish are resilient little creatures. They're essentially floating blobs of H2O, drifting around like nature's water balloons, which makes them the ocean's least hydrated but still totally functional creatures.

BONUS FUNNY FUN FACT

Arm Yourself!

When you lose an arm, just grow a new one!

The starfish is a true champion of regeneration. If it loses an arm (whether due to a predator or an accident), it doesn't just cry about it—it regrows the lost limb! In fact, some starfish species can even grow a completely new starfish from a single arm. It's like having an endless supply of extra limbs, meaning starfish are ready for anything—be it a tough situation or just the next time they need to do the wave at a beach party.

Chapter 3: Food Facts That Are Both Weird and Wonderful (5 Facts)

Delicious Discoveries That Will Blow Your Mind (And Your Taste Buds)

Bananas are radioactive? Avocados are berries? These facts about food will have you questioning everything about your daily meals. And, trust us, it's a feast of weirdness. This chapter dives into the wild world of food, uncovering strange truths and shocking secrets about the things we put in our mouths every day.

Apples Float on Water

The Buoyant Apple

Gravity might be real, but apples defy it in style.

When you bob for apples, you're not just having fun—you're also witnessing a natural phenomenon. Apples float on water because they are made up of 25% air. That's why they bob in a water-filled bowl or pond. So, if you're ever stuck at a pool party with a bunch of apples and no bowls, just toss them into the water—they'll do their thing. This means the apple you're eating has the magical ability to float in water, but still somehow makes it into your stomach. Talk about multi-tasking!

The Glow-Up Banana

Your daily snack might just be giving off a little glow.

Bananas are not just a great source of potassium—they're also a little bit radioactive. They contain a tiny amount of potassium-40, a naturally occurring isotope. While it's true that this radiation is harmless and incredibly low (don't worry, you won't glow in the dark), it's still hilarious to think that the fruit that's so healthy could have a secret radioactive side. So next time you peel a banana, just remember: you're eating a snack that's both good for you and a little dangerous in the coolest way possible!

The Royal Carrot

The carrot revolutionized its color game.

Carrots today are mostly orange, but they didn't start out that way. The original carrots were purple, red, and even white. The orange variety we know today was cultivated in the 17th century by Dutch farmers as a tribute to the royal House of Orange. They were simply trying to show some loyalty! But today, the orange carrot reigns supreme, though purple carrots still pop up on occasion. So, next time you crunch into a carrot, just know you're eating a little piece of history—and probably something royal.

Ketchup Was Once Sold as Medicine

The Secret Healing Powers of Ketchup

Ketchup: The miracle cure of the 1800s.

What's more ridiculous than the fact that ketchup was once sold as a cure-all medicine? In the 1830s, Dr. John Cook Bennett promoted ketchup as a remedy for indigestion, claiming that its tomatoes were packed with health benefits. He even sold it in pill form! While we can't say we'd recommend using ketchup as medicine, we can appreciate that it was at least creative. So the next time you're feeling off, you might want to skip the bottle of ketchup and go for some actual medicine—unless you're just really craving fries.

Honey Never Spoils

Sweet Forever

The world's only snack that lasts longer than your shelf life.

This one's a little sweeter than most: honey never spoils. Archaeologists have discovered pots of honey in ancient Egyptian tombs that are still perfectly edible after thousands of years. How does it last so long? The low moisture content and acidic pH create an inhospitable environment for bacteria and microorganisms. So, if you ever find a jar of honey tucked away in the back of your pantry, don't throw it out—it's still good to go! Honey is the timeless snack, always ready for your tea or toast.

Pineapples Were Once So Expensive, They Were Rented Out

The Pineapple Premium

When pineapples were the status symbol of luxury.

Everyone loves avocados—on toast, in guacamole, or just by the spoonful. But did you know that technically, avocados are berries? That's right! Botanically speaking, they belong to the berry family, which includes other fruits like bananas and pumpkins. So, the next time you add some guac to your chips, just think: you're munching on a berry, not a vegetable. Avocados are out here defying expectations—and your grocery list.

Avocados Are Actually Berries

The Berry That's a Fruit Impostor

Avocados might be fooling you with their savory nature.

Everyone loves avocados—on toast, in guacamole, or just by the spoonful. But did you know that technically, avocados are berries? That's right! Botanically speaking, they belong to the berry family, which includes other fruits like bananas and pumpkins. So, the next time you add some guac to your chips, just think: you're munching on a berry, not a vegetable. Avocados are out here defying expectations—and your grocery list.

Chapter 4: Things That Are Just Plain Bizarre (5 Facts)

The Weirdest Realities That'll Make You Question Everything

If you think the world makes sense, think again! This chapter is packed with facts so strange, you'll wonder if you've accidentally stepped into an alternate dimension. Why does the Eiffel Tower grow in the summer? How do clouds stay so fluffy? Get ready for some mind-bending, laugh-out-loud absurdities that will turn your view of the world upside down.

FUNNY FUN FACT #18

The Eiffel Tower Can Grow Taller in the Summer

The Eiffel Tower's Seasonal Growth Spurt

Who knew a tower could have growth spurts?

It's not a joke, it's the real deal! The Eiffel Tower grows taller in the summer. Due to the heat, the metal expands, and the iconic structure can grow by up to 6 inches. Imagine your favorite tower just getting taller whenever it feels like it. I mean, can you imagine your house randomly getting 6 inches taller when it's hot outside? Talk about a building with a bit of a "growth spurt complex!"

FUNNY FUN FACT #19

There's a Hotel Made of Ice That You Can Sleep In

Winter Wonderland—Made of Ice!

Feel like a snowman as you sleep in a solid ice room.

Ever wanted to sleep in a room made entirely of ice? Well, the IceHotel in Sweden makes it possible. The hotel is made of snow and ice, and everything—from the furniture to the chandeliers—is frozen. Guests sleep in thermal sleeping bags to stay warm. Who knew being cold could be this luxurious?

FUNNY FUN FACT #20

A Cow's Moo Is a Personal Sound

Cow-llaboration of Moo-sic

No two cows sound alike—every moo is unique!

Believe it or not, every cow's moo is unique, just like human fingerprints. Cows actually moo in a way that's tailored to their specific voice, making them the divas of the barnyard. It's like each moo is a personalized tune for every cow, just waiting to make its mark on the world. I guess cows could start a whole new genre of music—Moo-sic! Let's hope there's no moo-sical rivalry among the cows.

It Rains Fish in Honduras

Fishy Weather Forecast

Forget snow or rain, Honduras gets fish!

Once or twice a year, a strange phenomenon called "Lluvia de Peces" (Rain of Fish) occurs in Honduras, where fish literally fall from the sky. Scientists believe this happens due to tornado-like winds pulling the fish up from nearby rivers and dumping them down on the towns. You could get soaked by a storm of fish—talk about a "catch of the day!"

FUNNY FUN FACT #22

There's a City Named Dull, and It's Paired with Boring

The Dull and Boring Pairing

The most exciting relationship you'll ever hear of.

In the UK, there is a town named Dull in Scotland, and it just so happens to be paired with a town called Boring in Oregon, USA. Together, they form the "Dull and Boring" connection. Now that's a pair of places with a seriously fun name! What's next—"Tedious" and "Monotonous"?

A Cloud Can Weigh More Than a Million Pounds

The Heavy Weight of Clouds

Who knew clouds were so heavy?

A typical cloud can weigh as much as 1 million pounds—that's heavier than 100 full-grown elephants! It may look fluffy and light, but clouds are made of tiny water droplets that add up to some serious weight. Don't worry, though—the air is buoyant enough to keep them floating up there.

You Can Pay to Have Your Name Sent to Mars

Your Name, the Martian Way

The ultimate space souvenir—no spacesuit required!

Here's an offer you can't refuse: For free, you can have your name sent to Mars via a NASA mission! While you won't be physically traveling to Mars, your name will travel there aboard a spacecraft, making it the ultimate space souvenir. Who knew interplanetary bragging rights were so accessible?

You Can Lick Your Elbow (But Only If You're Lucky)

The Elbow-Licking Challenge

Try it—if you can!

It's an age-old challenge—can you lick your elbow? Turns out, a very small percentage of people (around 1 in 20) can actually pull it off. Your body is just not built for it, but it's fun to try! Next time you're bored, test your flexibility and see if you're one of the lucky few. If not, well, at least you had a good laugh!

Your Belly Button Is Home to More Bacteria Than People on Earth

Your Belly Button: A Personal Bacteria Resort

The ultimate hotspot for bacteria—more popular than the entire planet!

Your belly button is secretly one of the busiest places on your body, hosting more bacteria than there are people on Earth. In fact, scientists estimate that the average belly button holds around 2,000 species of bacteria. So, your belly button is basically like the VIP section of the microbial world. Who knew it was such a hotspot?

Chapter 5: The Funniest Human Facts You'll Ever Hear (5 Facts)

Humans: The Species That Can't Stop Being Ridiculous

Oh, humans. We've created space travel, but we've also managed to make a mess out of the simplest things. From quirky world records to hilarious historical events, this chapter shines a light on the wonderfully ridiculous ways we get things hilariously wrong. If you thought we were the smartest species, these facts will prove we're also the funniest!

In 2011, a Woman Tried to Pay for McDonald's with a Live Alligator

Would You Like Gator with That?

When Fast Food Meets Wild Payment Methods

"In 2011, a woman in Florida tried to pay for McDonald's with a live alligator. Talk about a 'happy meal' surprise!"

Only in Florida! In a bizarre twist of events in 2011, a woman pulled up to a McDonald's drive-thru and offered an unusual form of payment—a live 3.5-foot alligator. Whether she thought the cashier needed a new pet or was bartering for Big Macs is still unclear, but authorities were called, and the gator made a swift getaway (to wildlife officials). McDonald's didn't accept the scaly currency, but the story proves that life's full of surprises—and questionable decisions!

FUNNY FUN FACT #24

The Oldest Joke in the World is a Bathroom Joke

4,000 Years of Potty Humor

Proof That Toilet Humor is Timeless

"The oldest joke known to humanity is over 4,000 years old, and yes, it's about bathroom humor. Some things never change."

Discovered in ancient Sumer, the first recorded joke proves that humans have always found bathroom-related topics hilarious. The joke involves a married woman and, well, bathroom habits. This timeless humor shows that even 4,000 years ago, people enjoyed a good laugh over the most basic of human experiences.

In 2007, a Man Robbed a Bank with a Beehive

Heist That Really Stung

When Crime Meets Nature's Buzz

"A man attempted to rob a bank by threatening to unleash a swarm of bees from a live hive."

This criminal thought he could weaponize bees to secure his loot. He brandished a buzzing beehive at terrified bank employees, demanding money. Unfortunately for him, the police were quick to respond, and the "sticky" situation ended with him in custody. The bees were left wondering what all the fuss was about.

A Man Tried to Clone Himself in the 18th Century

A Mad Scientist Before His Time

When Curiosity Got the Best of Him

"In the 1700s, an eccentric man attempted to clone himself using primitive methods and a lot of imagination."

Well before modern science understood genetics, one man in the 18th century decided to replicate himself. His methods were questionable (and completely ineffective), but his ambition set the tone for what would later become a sci-fi reality. Was it science, or just pure vanity? You decide.

Napoleon Was Once Attacked by a Horde of Bunnies

The Emperor's Fluffy Downfall

Cute but Surprisingly Aggressive

"Napoleon Bonaparte once organized a rabbit hunt, but the rabbits turned the tables and attacked him instead."

:

In a bizarre turn of events, Napoleon planned a grand rabbit hunt with hundreds of bunnies. Instead of fleeing, the bunnies charged at him and his men, forcing the emperor to make a hasty retreat. History books rarely mention it, but fluffy rebellion is real!

Chapter 6: Funny Facts About Our Earth and Beyond (5 Facts)

Welcome to Earth (or Maybe Not)

Earth might be our home, but it's definitely not as normal as we like to think. Whether it's Earth's strange superpowers or the hilarious truths about our planet's oddities, this chapter will have you laughing—and maybe wondering if we're all just living in the weirdest science experiment ever. And when we look beyond our planet? Well, the universe is even stranger!

You Could Fit 1.8 Million Earths Inside the Sun

Earth? Tiny! Sun? HUGE!

How many Earths do you need to fill the Sun?

The Sun is so massive, you could fit 1.8 million Earths inside it. So, the next time you complain about your cramped living space, just remember: you're smaller than a single speck in the massive sun house! It's like trying to fill a football stadium with peas—if the football stadium were the size of a galaxy, of course. Maybe not the best idea to move in there, though—no oxygen and all.

FUNNY FUN FACT #29

A Day on Venus Is Longer Than a Year on Venus

Time Is All Relative on Venus

The planet where a day lasts longer than a year!

Venus has one of the most bizarre rotational patterns in the solar system. A day on Venus – the time it takes for the planet to rotate once on its axis – is 243 Earth days. But a year on Venus – the time it takes for Venus to orbit the Sun – is only 225 Earth days. So, on Venus, a day actually lasts longer than its year! If you were living on Venus, you'd have plenty of time to enjoy your "day" while the year just zooms by. Talk about taking your time with things!

There's a Giant Diamond in Space Called "Lucy"

Diamonds Are Forever... and 50 Light-Years Away

A Cosmic Rock Worth Billions

"A white dwarf star named BPM 37093 is a massive diamond, weighing 10 billion trillion carats. Bling for the galaxy!"

Nicknamed "Lucy" after The Beatles' song, this crystallized star core is the universe's largest jewel. Too bad it's 50 light-years away, or it could be the centerpiece of an interstellar engagement ring.

FUNNY FUN FACT #31

In Ancient Greece, Toothpaste Was Made From Urine

A Smile to Die For

Minty Fresh Wasn't a Thing

"The Greeks used human urine as a whitening agent for toothpaste. Don't worry—modern toothpaste has improved significantly!"

:

Ammonia, found in urine, was a key ingredient for ancient tooth care. Though effective, it's a relief that we've traded ancient remedies for minty gels. Imagine morning breath plus… that!

FUNNY FUN FACT #32

The First Toothbrush Was Made from Hog Hair

A Hairy History of Oral Hygiene

When Brushing Your Teeth Was a Lot More Uncomfortable

""The first toothbrush was made from hog hair. So, if you ever feel weird about your hairbrush, remember: it used to be much worse!"

:

The very first toothbrush, dating back to the 15th century in China, was crafted using hog hair bristles. Imagine using a rough, bristly brush made from pig hair to clean your teeth! It wasn't exactly the soft, bristle-filled tools we enjoy today. While this early brush might sound a bit grim, it's a testament to how far dental hygiene has come. Modern toothbrushes are now a far cry from the discomfort of hog hair—thankfully!

Chapter 7: The World's Weirdest Records (6 Facts)

World Records You Didn't Know You Needed to Know

Who needs gold medals when you can hold a world record for doing something outrageously bizarre? This chapter brings you the weirdest, funniest, and most unexpected records that will leave you questioning how in the world these feats were even possible. Could you be the next champion of one of these truly unique categories? Only one way to find out!

Breaking Records with a Gaseous Gesture

When Burping Becomes a Competitive Sport

"The world record for the longest burp is 1 minute and 13 seconds—sounds like someone really enjoyed that soda!"

Burps are natural, but this man took it to the next level. The world record for the longest burp is held by a man named Paul Hunn, who managed to burp continuously for 1 minute and 13 seconds! While many might consider this a natural bodily function, Paul turned it into a competitive event. Now that's a record to celebrate (or cringe at)!

FUNNY FUN FACT #34

Most T-Shirts Worn at Once

Clothing, but Make It Extreme

When Fashion Goes Too Far

"The world record for wearing the most T-shirts at once is 257. That's one way to avoid laundry day!"

:

Who needs a wardrobe full of options when you can just wear every T-shirt you own at once? That's exactly what Sanath Bandara did when he set the world record for wearing 257 T-shirts. He's now probably the most well-protected person against cold weather—though we'd love to see him try to go through a door or sit down. Talk about a tight fit!

Most Toothpicks Stuck in a Beard

The Unusual Art of Beard Decoration

When Beard Grooming Gets Out of Hand

"The record for most toothpicks stuck in a beard is 3,500. It's like the beard version of a porcupine!"

If you've ever wondered if it's possible to take beard grooming too far, think no more. Axel Rosales proved it's possible by sticking 3,500 toothpicks in his beard, setting the world record. Now, his beard looks more like a giant hedgehog than facial hair. And while his grooming technique is certainly creative, we're not sure it's the best way to keep your beard looking sharp!

FUNNY FUN FACT #36

Most Nails Pounded Into Wood in One Minute

Hammering Home the Point

When Speed and Power Combine in an Odd Way

"The world record for the most nails pounded into wood in one minute is 72. Talk about getting to the point!"

In the category of weird skills, Jack Harris is a true champion. His world record of pounding 72 nails into wood in just one minute is not only fast but also incredibly impressive. With a hammer in hand, Jack's got some serious force behind his strikes—proof that when it comes to breaking records, sometimes you just have to hit the nail on the head... repeatedly!

The Quirky Obsession with Floating Toys

Quack-tastic Collecting

"The world's largest collection of rubber ducks is 9,000. Who knew they were so collectible?"

Charlotte Lee from the USA holds the world record for having the largest collection of rubber ducks—9,000 of them! From classic yellow ducks to uniquely designed ones, her collection is a sight to behold. And while most of us might have one or two floating around in our bathrooms, Charlotte's obsession with these quirky creatures makes her the undisputed queen of rubber duckies!

Longest Pizza Delivery

Pizza, but Make It Global

A Slice of Life Across the Globe

"The longest pizza delivery was 13,000 kilometers. Now that's what you call going the extra mile for pizza!"

When it comes to pizza, there are no boundaries—Domino's Pizza proved that by delivering a pizza over 13,000 kilometers from Italy to Australia. This massive pizza delivery wasn't just about satisfying a craving—it was a publicity stunt. The delivery took 1,000 years of pizza-making traditions across multiple countries, making it the longest pizza delivery in history. And it definitely wasn't your average fast food!

Chapter 8: Truly Useless (But Hilarious) Knowledge (5 Facts)

Knowledge You'll Forget in 5 Minutes (But It Was Funny While It Lasted)

We've all heard the saying, "You can't take it with you." Well, this chapter is filled with knowledge you won't remember 10 minutes after reading—but you'll definitely get a good laugh while it lasts. These bizarre, funny, and utterly random facts are perfect for impressing (and confusing) your friends at the next party. Just don't expect to retain any of it. It's all about the fun in the moment!

FUNNY FUN FACT #39

You Can't Hum While Holding Your Nose

Try it out!

I bet you can't do it!!!

It's scientifically impossible to hum while holding your nose. The air needs to come out of your nose to create the humming sound, and well, your nose is blocked. Go ahead and try—it's hilarious to watch.

Next time someone tells you to hum a tune, try plugging your nose and see what happens. You'll quickly find out that humming while blocking your nostrils is impossible because the air needs to pass through your nose to create the sound. It's a fun and simple experiment to try, and it might leave you laughing at how basic biology works.

FUNNY FUN FACT #40

The Shortest War in History Lasted 38 Minutes

Talk about a quick battle!

Blink, and You Missed It!

The Anglo-Zanzibar War of 1896 holds the record for the shortest war in history, lasting just 38 minutes. A true testament to how quickly things can go wrong!

The Anglo-Zanzibar War took place on August 27, 1896, between the British Empire and the Sultanate of Zanzibar. The conflict lasted only 38 minutes, making it the shortest recorded war in history. The war was sparked when the sultan of Zanzibar, who had a pro-German stance, refused to step down after the British backed another candidate. With superior naval and military power, the British quickly overwhelmed the Zanzibari forces, bringing the conflict to a rapid and decisive end. In less time than it takes to have lunch, the shortest war in history was over!

A Group of Ravens is Called an Unkindness

Even Smart Birds Can Have a Bad Reputation

Ironically Unkind for Such Clever Creatures

Ravens gather in an unkindness, which is ironically unkind for such a smart bird.

Ravens are highly intelligent birds, known for their ability to use tools and communicate complex ideas. Despite their brilliance, a group of ravens is called an "unkindness." This name likely comes from ancient folklore, where ravens were often seen as omens of doom. It's ironic that such clever creatures would be associated with something so negative. So, while you may think of ravens as crafty and intelligent, don't let their group name fool you—they may be more thoughtful than their label suggests!

The Unicorn is Scotland's National Animal

A Mythical Beast Representing Scotland's Spirit

Scotland Embraces Fantasy in Its National Symbol

The unicorn is Scotland's national animal, which doesn't even exist!

Scotland's national animal is none other than the unicorn, a mythical creature that doesn't exist in real life. Chosen for its representation of purity, strength, and beauty, the unicorn has been a symbol of Scotland for centuries. This decision is a quirky and fantastical one, but it highlights Scotland's rich cultural heritage and its embrace of imagination and myth. While unicorns are only found in legends and fantasy, they hold a very real place in Scotland's heart.

The Cube Poop Mystery of Wombats

When nature gives you cubes instead of spheres.

Wombats produce cube-shaped poop, and it's one of the weirdest facts in the animal kingdom. Scientists believe that their intestines have a unique structure that allows them to shape their poop into perfect little cubes. These cubic droppings are thought to help mark their territory without rolling away. Next time you're struggling to pack your lunch, just remember: wombats have mastered the art of "packing" in a way that no human can quite replicate.

Chapter 9: Bizarre Space Facts (7 Facts)

The Universe is Bigger, Stranger, and More Hilarious Than You Think

Space—where the weirdness never ends. From planets that might just have the oddest weather to diamonds the size of Earth floating out there, the universe has a sense of humor that's out of this world. This chapter will give you a peek into the cosmic oddities that will have you laughing at the vastness of space (and possibly questioning if aliens are watching us with a good laugh, too).

FUNNY FUN FACT #44

There's a Giant Cloud of Alcohol in Space

The Universe's Boozy Secret

A Cosmic Cocktail Floating in Space

There's a giant cloud of alcohol in space—enough to make 400 trillion trillion pints of beer!

In space, there's a massive cloud of alcohol—specifically, ethyl alcohol—floating around. This cloud, which is located near the center of the Milky Way, contains enough alcohol to make about 400 trillion trillion pints of beer! Scientists discovered this cosmic cocktail while studying a massive star-forming region in the galaxy. While this alcohol is far too diffuse to drink, it does make you wonder if space could be the ultimate source of all the party supplies we need.

Space Smells Like Metal and Burnt Stea

The Weirdest Aroma in the Universe

The Final Frontier... With a Strange Scent

Space smells like burnt steak, hot metal, and welding fumes!

Astronauts have reported that space has a unique smell when they remove their helmets after spacewalks. The scent has been described as a mix of hot metal, burnt steak, and even a little bit like welding fumes. Scientists believe this smell comes from high-energy particles in space interacting with the material of the spacesuits. Either way, space has an aroma that's far from the fresh, clean air we're used to here on Earth!

FUNNY FUN FACT #46

There's a Planet Where It Rains Glass

A Planet with Dangerous, Shiny Showers

Get Ready for Some Brutal Weather

On the planet HD 189733b, it rains glass sideways—imagine being caught in a rainstorm like that!

HD 189733b is a planet located about 63 light-years from Earth, and it has some of the most extreme weather conditions in the universe. The planet experiences wind speeds of up to 5,400 miles per hour, which causes the rain to fall sideways in the form of molten glass. If you were ever unlucky enough to visit this planet, you'd need more than just an umbrella to survive—perhaps a full suit of armor! It's one of the strangest and most dangerous weather patterns found anywhere in the universe, turning an otherwise "beautiful" rainy day into a perilous situation.

The Messy Side of Saturn's Beautiful Rings

Snow Globe of Space Debris

The rings around Saturn aren't made of shiny, pretty jewels. They're mostly chunks of ice, rock, and space debris—basically, Saturn is wearing a huge, messy snow globe!

While Saturn's rings may look like a dazzling display of jewels, in reality, they're more like a cosmic snowstorm. Composed mainly of ice, rock, and dust particles, these rings are constantly changing and moving. Saturn's rings are the universe's biggest, dirtiest snow globe—an ongoing reminder that even the most beautiful things can be a little bit messy.

Venus Has a Day Longer Than a Year

The Planet With an Upside-Down Schedule

Venus Flips Time on Its Head

On Venus, a single day lasts longer than its year—meaning it takes Venus more time to rotate once on its axis than it does to orbit around the Sun!

Imagine living on a planet where a day stretches longer than a whole year! Venus defies our basic understanding of time. It takes Venus about 243 Earth days to complete one rotation, but only 225 Earth days to orbit the Sun. So, if you lived there, you'd experience more sunsets than birthdays. Talk about having a slow day!

A Day on Mercury is Longer Than Its Year

Time Works Differently on Mercury

Mercury's Confusing Time Schedule

On Mercury, a single day lasts about 59 Earth days, but it only takes 88 Earth days for it to complete a full orbit around the Sun. So, Mercury's day is longer than its year—talk about a slow start to the workday!

Mercury's day is a bizarre cosmic time loop. While it takes just 88 Earth days for the planet to make one full orbit around the Sun, a single rotation on Mercury (a day) takes a mind-boggling 59 Earth days! So if you were working there, you'd find yourself stuck in an endless loop of waking up, getting a cup of coffee, and then it's time to go to bed again—without ever finishing a year!

The Biggest Thing in the Universe is Invisible

The Universe's Largest Mystery

Something So Huge, We Can't Even See It

The largest thing in the universe is a supermassive black hole, and it's so massive, we can't even see it!

 The biggest thing in the universe isn't a planet, star, or galaxy. It's a supermassive black hole, and it can be millions or even billions of times the mass of the Sun. The catch? You can't see it because it doesn't let any light escape. It's so large that it swallows everything in its vicinity, but we can only detect it through its gravitational pull. So, it's basically the universe's biggest celebrity... just totally invisible!

Chapter 10: The Final Laugh

One Last Gasp of Ridiculousness

You've laughed, you've learned, and now we're sending you off with the ultimate punchline. This chapter pulls together the strangest, most hilarious facts that are guaranteed to have you rolling on the floor. You've made it this far, so buckle up for one last burst of fun, because we're finishing strong with the weirdest, wackiest tidbits to leave you in stitches!

One Last Gasp of Ridiculousness

You've made it to the end of this hilariously bizarre journey through the weirdest, funniest, and most outlandish facts in the world. From mind-bending animal abilities to ridiculous records and space oddities, we've laughed our way through it all. But don't worry, we're not letting you off that easily. You've earned one final laugh before we wrap up this epic collection of the funniest fun facts!

So sit back, relax, and prepare for the ultimate punchline. This chapter will leave you laughing, questioning your reality, and wondering how you lived your life without knowing the hilariously weird truths we've shared. It's like that perfect ending to a comedy show—just when you think it's over, we hit you with one last gut-buster!

The Final Laugh
And now, the ultimate "weird" fact to send you off with a smile. You've made it through all these wacky truths, and now it's time to ask the most important question of all:

Why did the astronaut break up with his girlfriend?
Because he needed space!

Ba dum tss!

Alright, alright—maybe it wasn't that funny. But hey, it's the thought that counts, right? And just like that, we wrap up your journey through the land of hilarious and weird facts. If you got a chuckle out of that space joke, then our mission is complete. If not, well, don't worry. We've learned that humor is all about timing—and in the case of this book, timing means cramming as many bizarre truths as possible into one awesome ride.

But here's the thing: you can always come back to this book when you need a good laugh, a fun fact, or just a reason to share some absurdity with the world. You've earned the title of fun fact expert, so go out there and show off what you've learned. Who knew the universe was this ridiculous?

Conclusion: The Only Thing We Can Guarantee? More Laughter

The End… But Just the Beginning of More Laughs

Well, you've made it to the end—and we hope you've been laughing all the way through. But don't worry, the fun isn't over. We're only getting started. If you didn't laugh at least once, we might've failed. But we know you'll be back for more—because these facts are just too good to forget!

Thank You for Joining Us on This Ridiculous Journey!

Well, we've reached the end of our crazy ride through the world of funny facts, absurd truths, and laugh-out-loud revelations. By now, you're probably questioning how you went through life without knowing that wombat poop is cube-shaped or that a unicorn is Scotland's national animal. But don't worry, you're not alone—now you're equipped with the most bizarre and hilarious facts to share with friends, family, and anyone who needs a good laugh. You can thank us later.

What's Next for You?
Now that you've survived the wild ride of ridiculous facts, the next step is simple: Share these gems with the world! Whether you drop them in casual conversation, pull them out during trivia night, or impress your friends with your deep knowledge of the weird and wonderful, you're now a certified fun fact expert.

But don't stop there—these facts are more than just conversation starters. They are your secret weapons for winning arguments, impressing first dates, or making the most boring family gathering a little more entertaining. You're armed with enough absurd knowledge to keep everyone around you giggling for years to come.

Want to Test Your New Fun Fact Expertise?
Now that you've become a master of hilarious facts, it's time for the ultimate challenge: Take the quiz!

You've read these fun facts, but can you remember them all? The quiz will test your knowledge and give you a chance to prove just how much of a fun fact champion you've become. Who knows? You might even score a perfect 100 and earn the title of "Fun Fact Guru of the Year." We'll just go ahead and say it: It's a prestigious title that comes with unlimited bragging rights!

Thank You for Joining Us on This Ridiculous Journey!

So go ahead—take the quiz and show off your new superpower. And if you don't score as high as you hoped? No worries—just consider it an excuse to re-read the book and enjoy more laughs.

Laughing is the Best Medicine
We've all heard the saying, "Laughter is the best medicine," and we can't help but agree. Whether you're having a bad day, need a mood boost, or simply want to make your friends roll their eyes at how ridiculous you can be, these fun facts have got you covered.

Plus, let's face it: when you learn something as ridiculous as Mercury's day being longer than its year, how can you not laugh? The universe is a weird place, and we're just lucky to live in it—one laugh at a time.

So, next time you're feeling down, just remember the timeless wisdom of this book: Laughter is the best way to deal with the chaos of life.

The Power of Sharing Laughter
The truth is, the world can be a strange place, but humor has the power to bring us all together. It's universal. It's uplifting. And it's contagious. You've just unlocked a treasure chest of fun facts, and it's your duty to spread the joy. Share these wild truths, laugh at the ridiculousness, and let the ripple effect of giggles continue to expand.

You never know when one of these wacky facts will be exactly what someone needs to hear.

Thank You for Joining Us on This Ridiculous Journey!

In Conclusion, Here's a Parting Joke to Keep the Laughter Rolling:
Why don't skeletons fight each other?
Because they don't have the guts!

A Final Thank You!
Before you go, we just want to say thank you for being a part of this adventure.
You've explored, laughed, and discovered the weirdest truths about our world.
And remember—just because you've finished this book doesn't mean the fun has
to stop. Keep coming back to these facts whenever you need a good laugh or
want to impress the next group of people you encounter.

As we like to say, Life's too short to take seriously. So laugh, share, and embrace
the weirdness!

End Note:
Now go forth, fellow fun-fact champion. The world is full of weird, wonderful,
and totally hilarious facts, and you're ready to share them with everyone you
meet. Who knows? You might just start the next big laugh trend. Keep it weird,
keep it funny, and keep on laughing!

And remember: Take the quiz and prove you're the true fun fact king (or queen)!

Bonus: The Funniest Fun Facts Quiz

Test Your Knowledge and Laugh Along the Way

Think you've remembered all the crazy, hilarious facts you just read? Time to put your knowledge to the test with this fun quiz! Don't worry, it's not a pop quiz—just a lighthearted challenge to see how many of these bizarre and funny facts have stuck with you. Ready to see how much you've learned? (And how much you can laugh at the process!) Grab your pen, and let's see if you can ace it—or at least have a good laugh trying!

Funniest Fun Facts Quiz

Questions

1.What animal can punch like a bullet and break glass?
A) Elephant
B) Mantis Shrimp
C) Gorilla
D) Kangaroo

2.Which planet has a day that lasts longer than its year?
A) Venus
B) Mercury
C) Earth
D) Mars

3.What fruit is classified as a berry, despite its size?
A) Apple
B) Banana
C) Avocado
D) Kiwi

4.What animal's poop is shaped like cubes?
A) Kangaroo
B) Wombat
C) Elephant
D) Lion

5.Which country's national animal is the unicorn?
A) Ireland
B) United Kingdom
C) Scotland
D) Iceland

6.What animal has the ability to breathe through its butt?
A) Duck
B) Sea Cucumber
C) Octopus
D) Frog

7.Which planet rains glass sideways?
A) Mars
B) Saturn
C) HD 189733b
D) Jupiter

Funniest Fun Facts Quiz

8.Which of these animals have "best friends"?
A) Cows
B) Pigs
C) Goats
D) Monkeys

9.What animal can live for 200 years or more?
A) Elephant
B) Whale
C) Tortoise
D) Shark

10.Which animal is known to have a "flamboyance" of its kind?
A) Flamingo
B) Penguin
C) Ostrich
D) Peacock

11.Which human being attempted to clone himself in the 18th century?
A) Isaac Newton
B) Benjamin Franklin
C) Giovanni Aldini
D) Thomas Jefferson

12.Which of the following animals can sleep with one eye open?
A) Dolphin
B) Owl
C) Shark
D) Elephant

13.What fruit can be radioactive due to the potassium it contains?
A) Tomato
B) Banana
C) Orange
D) Apple

14.What animal can punch with such force that it can shatter shells?
A) Mantis Shrimp
B) Tiger
C) Gorilla
D) Octopus

Funniest Fun Facts Quiz

15. **Which country's Eiffel Tower grows in the summer?**
A) France
B) Germany
C) Italy
D) Spain

16.**What planet is known for its rings, which are mostly ice, rock, and debris?**
A) Earth
B) Saturn
C) Uranus
D) Neptune

17.**Which of the following is not a berry, despite being commonly referred to as one?**
A) Strawberry
B) Raspberry
C) Blueberry
D) Banana

18.**In what year did a man rob a bank with a live beehive?**
A) 2005
B) 2007
C) 2010
D) 2008

19.**Which planet has weather so extreme it rains glass?**
A) Venus
B) Saturn
C) HD 189733b
D) Mars

20.**What animal uses human urine as toothpaste?**
A) Ancient Greeks
B) Ancient Romans
C) Egyptians
D) Vikings

21.**What is the first toothbrush made from?**
A) Plastic
B) Animal Hair
C) Wood
D) Bone

Funniest Fun Facts Quiz

22. What country has a unicorn as its national animal?
A) Scotland
B) Ireland
C) Canada
D) Norway

23.What type of animal is known to have "best friends"?
A) Dolphins
B) Cows
C) Gorillas
D) Parrots

24.What planet is known for its extreme temperature swings, where it rains glass?
A) Mars
B) Neptune
C) HD 189733b
D) Venus

25.Which animal is known for "dancing" to communicate?
A) Bees
B) Birds
C) Kangaroos
D) Frogs

26.What type of animal is capable of breathing through its butt?
A) Duck
B) Sea Cucumber
C) Octopus
D) Frog

27.What fruit has seeds on the outside, making it technically not a true fruit?
A) Pear
B) Strawberry
C) Banana
D) Pineapple

28.What animal uses rocks as tools to break into clams?
A) Dolphins
B) Chimpanzees
C) Otters
D) Seals

29.Which animal produces cube-shaped poop?
A) Koala
B) Wombat
C) Armadillo
D) Kangaroo

Funniest Fun Facts Quiz

30. Which planet has the longest days in the solar system?
A) Venus
B) Mercury
C) Mars
D) Jupiter

31. What animal has a "superpower" of punching at 50 miles per hour?
A) Mantis Shrimp
B) Gorilla
C) Cheetah
D) Kangaroo

32. Which animal sleeps with one eye open to stay alert?
A) Dolphin
B) Owl
C) Shark
D) Bear

33.Which planet has a day that lasts longer than a year?
A) Venus
B) Earth
C) Mars
D) Mercury

34.Which of these animals have been known to form long-lasting friendships?
A) Monkeys
B) Dogs
C) Cows
D) Rabbits

35.What planet has rings made of ice and space debris?
A) Neptune
B) Saturn
C) Jupiter
D) Uranus

36.Which of these animals has been recorded to live for over 200 years?
A) Elephant
B) Tortoise
C) Whale
D) Shark

37.What food is technically a berry, despite its unusual size and shape?
A) Tomato
B) Kiwi
C) Avocado
D) Banana

Funniest Fun Facts Quiz

38.What animal has been found to have "best friends" within its species?
A) Cows
B) Sheep
C) Dogs
D) Cats

39. Which animal has a poop shaped like cubes?
A) Wombat
B) Koala
C) Kangaroo
D) Armadillo

40.What planet experiences extreme temperature swings, ranging from super hot to super cold?
A) Venus
B) Mercury
C) Mars
D) Neptune

41.What vegetable is often mistaken for a fruit, but is technically not?
A) Tomato
B) Carrot
C) Avocado
D) Cucumber

42.Which planet has a year that is shorter than its day?
A) Mercury
B) Venus
C) Earth
D) Mars

43.Which country has a national animal that is a mythical creature?
A) Scotland
B) Iceland
C) New Zealand
D) Canada

44.Which animal is known for making a "flamboyance" when it's in a group?
A) Flamingo
B) Peacock
C) Tiger
D) Penguin

Funniest Fun Facts Quiz

45.Which of these animals can hold its breath longer than most human divers?
A) Dolphin
B) Whale
C) Sea Lion
D) Crocodile

46.Which planet has extreme weather that includes glass rain?
A) Venus
B) Mars
C) HD 189733b
D) Saturn

47.Which fruit is radioactive due to its potassium content?
A) Banana
B) Apple
C) Pear
D) Peach

48.What animal can break glass with the force of its punch?
A) Mantis Shrimp
B) Gorilla
C) Tiger
D) Kangaroo

49.Which planet has such extreme weather that it rains glass sideways?
A) Mars
B) Venus
C) HD 189733b
D) Earth

50.Which planet is known for its rings that are made of icy debris and space rocks?
A) Jupiter
B) Saturn
C) Uranus
D) Neptune

The Ultimate Funny Fun Facts Quiz Scoring System

You've made it to the scoring section of the quiz, where we take your knowledge of ridiculous facts and turn it into something amusing. Let's see where you fall, and most importantly—let's have fun with it!

Point System

Correct Answer (2 points):
You nailed it! If you selected the right answer, you get a solid 2 points. Consider this the equivalent of winning a mini lottery—nothing life-changing, but it sure feels good. You're showing the world you're a fun fact aficionado. The more points, the more serious your fun fact game becomes! Keep it up!

Total Points Calculation

Let's see how well you did! Based on your score, here's how we'll break it down:

90–100 points (Excellent):

"Wow, you're a true Fun Fact Champion! You've crushed this quiz like a pro! You know more about bizarre facts than we ever imagined, and we're considering making you our official fun fact guru. You're basically a walking encyclopedia with a sense of humor. If this were a fun fact Olympics, you'd get the gold medal and a confetti shower. Don't be surprised if you start getting calls from trivia shows!"

70–89 points (Good):

"Nice work! You're like the runner-up in the fun fact trivia world—still amazing, but there's a little room for improvement. You knew most of the answers and got some real brain-busters, but there's still some trivia treasure to uncover. Think of yourself as the second-place pie-eating champ—you did great, but you didn't finish first. Next time, go for the gold star!"

50–69 points (Decent):

"You got through the quiz like a trooper—close, but not quite at the finish line. You knew your facts, but there were a few questions that threw you off. It's like when you binge-watch half a Netflix series and then skip the rest of the episodes. You were so close, but missed a couple of those tricky moments. Don't worry, we're cheering you on—try again and maybe bring some popcorn!"

Less than 50 points (Needs Work):

"Uh-oh, did you snooze through the quiz? Or was there a moment when you decided to start guessing wildly? Don't worry, we believe in you! A few more fun facts under your belt and you'll be the ultimate trivia master in no time. You've got the spirit, now just add a little more reading and a dash more silly knowledge, and you'll be on top next time. Keep your head up, you've got this!"

Now, Go Celebrate Your Score!
Whether you're a fun fact guru or a novice, remember: this quiz is all about having a laugh! So no matter your score, give yourself a round of applause, share some laughs with friends, and come back whenever you feel like proving your fun fact knowledge!

Funniest Fun Facts Quiz

Answer Key:

1. B) Mantis Shrimp
2. A) Venus
3. C) Avocado
4. B) Wombat
5. C) Scotland
6. B) Sea Cucumber
7. C) HD 189733b
8. B) Cows
9. C) Tortoise
10. A) Flamingo
11. C) Giovanni Aldini
12. A) Dolphin
13. B) Banana
14. A) Mantis Shrimp
15. A) France
16. B) Saturn
17. B) Strawberry
18. A) 2005
19. C) HD 189733b
20. A) Ancient Greeks
21. B) Animal Hair
22. A) Scotland
23. B) Dolphins
24. C) HD 189733b
25. A) Bees
26. B) Sea Cucumber
27. B) Strawberry
28. C) Otters
29. B) Wombat
30. A) Venus
31. A) Mantis Shrimp
32. A) Dolphin
33. A) Venus
34. C) Cows
35. B) Saturn
36. B) Tortoise
37. C) Avocado
38. A) Cows
39. A) Wombat
40. B) Mercury
41. A) Tomato
42. A) Mercury
43. A) Scotland
44. A) Flamingo
45. A) Dolphin
46. C) HD 189733b
47. A) Banana
48. A) Mantis Shrimp
49. C) HD 189733b
50. B) Saturn